DON'T
BE
Afraid
OF THE
DARK

BY SHANTINA MULLINS

Published by:
Your Vision Told
PO Box 613211
Dallas, TX 75261

Cover and layout design by Designed By Evelyn.
www.DesignedByEvelyn.com

ISBN-13: 978-1984964632
ISBN-10: 1984964631

MY WHY

The purpose of this book is to share my story and create awareness of mental wholeness and self-love. This can serve as a refreshing tool to help you overcome any obstacle and live the best life you truly deserve.

**"If there is no enemy within,
the enemy outside can do us no harm."
– Les Brown**

DEDICATION

This book is dedicated to my closest family and friends, thank you for all your support. Special thanks to my loving husband Lem, for your unwavering strength and always having my back. To my beautiful children Nia, Laila and Liam, you are the best part of me. To my girl Carra, thank you for pushing me to write. I finally put in a book. Lol

Contents

CHAPTER 1
THE DARK SIDE

Were you afraid of the dark as a child? Are you still afraid of it now? When I say the dark, I don't mean the dark literally, but symbolically speaking of the dark areas of your life or your dark side. The ones we know are there, but are afraid to confront. I remember having a lot of fears as a child, and many of those fears carried over into my adult life. My dark side was filled with deep rooted hurt, anger, depression, fear, anxiety, even suicidal thoughts. Most of the time no one even knew I was going through any of this. I hid it well for the most part. But, I was longing for someone to see inside me and help. My depression was also coupled with a deep root of rejection and abandonment which caused a fear of rejection, a fear of not being loved, never feeling good enough and worthless. I also carried a heavy weight of guilt, shame, and low self-esteem and lots of insecurities.

When we were young we were afraid of the dark because it represented the unknown or things that could possibly hurt us. But, when we turned the lights on we realized the unknown things were not so scary and it was just F.E.A.R. (false evidence appearing real). It's the same way as it relates to our dark side. It's filled with things we may not understand or are ashamed of, and which makes us afraid and so we hide it. It may be fear of dealing with something bigger or more painful than we're ready to handle; or fearing that if someone ever saw that side of us they would think we're really crazy. But, more people deal with a dark side than are willing to admit it. And because we're afraid to turn on the light, it continues to poison our life and decisions instead of empower us.

Yes, your dark side can either poison you or empower you. When we choose to hide it, it poisons our inner being, our thoughts, our actions, and it oozes out in the form of addictions, disorders, depression, anxiety, sickness, and other damaging results like a pattern of failed relationships or jobs, and so on. However, when we make a conscious choice to turn on the light, out of the darkness can come purpose, power and healing for yourself and others. Turning on the light involves healing from our earliest childhood wounds. It's a mix of exposing and understanding the dark and then inviting and embracing the light; slowly transforming into something new and rare and beautiful that would have never existed had it not endured the pain and pressure.

I grew up in Atlanta, Georgia. Initially, I was the middle child of three children and the only girl. My parents married young, or should I say my mother married my father young. As a young girl, I can remember there always being a lot of tension in our house. I used the word house intentionally, because it never felt like a home; I didn't feel safe. My father was an alcoholic which caused my parents to fight a lot. If they weren't arguing there were all-out brawls that lasted for what seemed like hours. Seeing your parents physically fight every day can leave a devastating effect on any child. I saw things young eyes should never see. I held a lot of it in most of the time. I remember running home from school every day praying my mom would still be alive, and being terrified that I would find her dead. I had nightmares many nights. I'll spare all the horrible details but my childhood was scary most days. I don't think anyone knew or even noticed what was going on in my home or my life. Through it all, I managed to make straight A's in school until around 8th grade when my father left for the second and last time. My parents were married and divorced twice. My brother and I begged my mom not to marry my dad the second time. So, when he left again I was relieved but little did I know that his leaving would drastically affect the rest of my life.

My family was very religious. It seemed like we were in church every day. My mom and dad prayed all the time, so why did I still feel like dying every day? I got the chicken pox during spring break when I was in the 9th grade and for some reason I was told "it messed up my equilibrium." I couldn't walk in a straight line without falling and my speech became slurred. I lost a part of my short-term memory and could barely write. I know that sounds weird but no one even knew what happened to me. We couldn't afford to go to the doctor so all my parents knew to do was pray. I think eventually I got better, but because I lost some of my short-term memory my grades at school began to slip. I was sad all the time and would sleep a lot in school. I didn't know what was going on with me or why. I just knew I wanted to escape everyday life. I would talk to God every night and ask Him not to wake me up the next morning. I remember feeling ugly and unloved and just constant hurt and sadness on the inside.

So, I became the class clown just to cope with the pain but it didn't stop the tears at night or fill the emptiness in my heart. My father noticed a change in me when he would come to visit. My room was usually very neat and clean but he noticed it was a dirty mess and my grades were either failing or barely passing. He sat me down and said my Aunt Red (his sister and the doctor in our family) said I was going through clinical depression and he asked if I wanted to talk about it. I said no. This was the first time I had heard the word depression, so it didn't make sense to me. Although my dad was trying to help me, I hated him because of how he treated my mom. So, I wouldn't listen to anything he had to say, good or bad. My mom thought I had a demon and would throw me on the bed trying to cast the spirit out of me, but nothing changed. She didn't understand and neither did I. Depressed? You must be crazy or have a demon and no child of mine gonna have a demon in my house.

Finally, during the summer of 10th grade, I think I went down for prayer at church and the next day I started to feel a lot better. I began to notice that I wasn't as depressed anymore. It was like a weight was lifted off me. But again, I still didn't understand what really happened.

I'm writing this book now at the age of 39, and I have had many episodes of depression throughout my life. However, before I go any further let me explain what depression is. Depression is intense sadness that lasts for an extended period of time; most of the time two weeks or more. It also comes with feelings of helplessness, hopelessness, guilt, shame, worthlessness, and loss of interest in activities you once loved. It can also affect your sleep patterns; some days you sleeping all day and others you're up all night. It also affects your eating habits; you can have an extended loss of appetite or overeat, which also causes significant weight loss or gain in a short period of time. You zone out staring off into space for a while and can't concentrate. You may even cry a lot. For me, I would feel like I had a monkey on my back that affected my daily activities.

I'm usually a go-getter, but when I was depressed I didn't feel like doing anything, so that's why my room would get messy and dirty. I would withdraw and wouldn't want to go out. I would go to work but I wouldn't want to go, so I'd start calling out and it would take me forever to get dressed. My thoughts and general outlook on life became extremely negative. I would become very pessimistic, irritable, cranky, and I couldn't see a way out my situation. I had a monkey on my back and a hole in my heart. I also had a hopeless outlook on life where I couldn't see a way out and that added to the sadness. When you are depressed, you feel helpless like there's no way out, or you can't be helped by anyone or anything. There are also levels of depression: mild, moderate, and severe. And I have been through them all. When you're severely depressed that's when the suicidal thoughts come. Anyone struggling with any level of depression, whether it's mild or severe, should seek professional help. But, unfortunately we are ashamed to ask for the help we truly need. And that is why I'm writing this book.

CHAPTER 2
WHAT'S YOUR TRIGGER?

I was driving to work one day and a song came on, Let it Snow, by Boyz II Men. Normally, this is a happy holiday song for most people. For me, it sent me driving down the street in tears. It triggered a painful memory from a devastating break-up.

A big part of dealing with depression is becoming aware of your triggers.

Triggers are things that cause or push you back into that dark place of depression or whatever your dark place is. My trigger was rejection, especially in the area of romantic relationships. Every Thanksgiving and Christmas holiday I would get extremely depressed because I was alone. I hated being alone. I felt like it reminded me of how unlovable I thought I was. When it got dark, it got really dark. Thoughts of suicide and in my lowest moments my emotions became so unbearable the only release I could feel was to cut myself, but I would always cover the wounds. I felt I was so unworthy of love that I would get angry and punch myself in the face and then feel ashamed and guilty afterward. No one really knew what I was going through. I mean how do you explain to someone that you hate yourself and that you punch yourself in the face?

On the outside I looked like everything was perfectly

fine--pretty makeup, nice clothes, cute hair, and temporary smiles to cover it all up. But, on the inside feeling like I'm dying a slow death and crying out "Somebody help me, somebody see me...see inside me. Fix me...Please!" I remember talking to a spiritual mentor about being depressed and having suicidal thoughts, and she really didn't know what to say and would say "Well, you look good." But, I was like "I feel horrible." Unless you've been through it you will never fully understand the war that goes on in your head when you're depressed.

I placed my value on my love relationships, and the lack of a romantic relationship just seemed to amplify the pain and feeling of not being loved and the feeling that I'm not enough. If I was in a relationship and things went downhill, usually because of cheating, that eventually ended in the demise of the love, and then the relationship was over. This opened the door to deep dark depression.

At 23 years old I attempted suicide.

I found out the guy I was dating cheated, and it broke me. It triggered pain I couldn't explain. We tried to work it out but the love and trust wasn't the same after that. Over one year's time, I lost my job, eventually my car, and then my relationship was falling apart. I also remember feeling I should end the relationship, but I think the fear of starting over stopped me from completely letting go. So, when he was finally done and wanted out of the relationship, I couldn't take that rush of unbearable pain. I ran to my bathroom and took a bottle of sleeping pills. I had bought the bottle because I was already depressed and finding it hard to sleep. He was leaving my apartment as I locked myself in the bathroom. He ran back in and busted the bathroom door open and realized what I had done and called 911. Immediately in the back of the ambulance I realized I did not want to die. I just wanted the pain to stop. I got really scared. I asked the paramedic if I was going to die and he said I should be ok because they got to me in time. They also noticed cuts on my arm. I lied and said I fell. Soon after we arrived at the emergency room I began to get sleepy. I stuck my finger down my throat and tried to make myself throw up but it didn't work. I screamed "Somebody help me please!" I then remember going to sleep and waking up and the nurses saying "drink this baby," and I would attempt to drink the charcoal they gave me and go back to sleep. The next day I had to go to the mental hospital. Let me pause here and say I did not want to go. I mean, isn't that for crazy people? But it was mandatory. I could hear something inside of me say *"Umm, yeah Tina, you just tried to take your life; you should pause for a minute and allow someone to help you."* But, a part of me still just wanted to get out of there and go home. There I was, a 23-year-old patient in the hospital for trying to take my life, and now I was headed to the psychiatric ward.

During my intake interview, I said I should have never tried to take my life and I wanted to live. Because I spoke strongly about living, they no longer felt I was a threat to myself and I got out the mental hospital the next day.

Upon my release from the hospital my best friend and I took a trip to get away and help reset my life. We went to NY for shopping and Miami to relax on the beach. The trips were a temporary solution, but it wasn't enough to stop the pain. When I got home and back to reality the hurt was still there. My mom and spiritual mentor called everyday to check on me but the feeling of abandonment still haunted me. The only difference was that I knew I wanted to live. But how?

I had no idea where to start or how to start living a better life. I still spent many nights crying myself to sleep, holding my Bible, and many nights saying "I will live and not die" aloud, because the pain was that excruciating. Now I had to find a solution. The only solution I knew of at that time was to spend time with God and ask Him for a solution. This is where I learned that depression is a symptom of an empty spirit, so I focused on filling my spirit. I was empty and I needed to fill up. And the more I thought about it, I was very empty. I was filled with shame from the break up, condemnation for the choices that led me there, and the sting of betrayal. But then, I could hear God speak to my spirit, saying that I was empty because I stopped using my weapon. And my voice was my weapon. He told me that in order to live again, I had to keep confessing His Word out of my mouth and make a choice never to stop.

Up until then, my mistake was that I actually believed the negative thoughts in my head. I didn't understand the power of my words and how they could transform my life. I allowed negative self-talk like "you're not supposed to be here, kill yourself" to just sit there in my head and fester, and eventually they became too much for me to handle. I didn't know at this time I needed to heal my soul. Now with this new Word and instruction from God to focus on my spirit, I was ready to move in the right direction. From that day on, I carved out time every morning not only to pray, but listen to a positive message, read my Word and positive books, and use my voice to say my affirmations every day. They had a new meaning in my life. This became my weapon and medicine and because I knew that, I took more responsibility in making sure I did this every day. I was not completely healed in one day but I could feel myself getting stronger and stronger each day.

Toxic Relationships

Toxic relationships are clearly a trigger to your dark side. So, if you're hanging around people who constantly hurt and disappoint you it's time to consider letting those relationships go. Easier said than done, I know. Especially if you are romantically involved with them. Or, if it's family, that makes it more complicated. Most of the time we expect from people something they just are not capable of giving us. But, we can choose to disconnect our expectations from them and put it back on God. Reading Psalms 62 often will help build this muscle. It states your expectation is of the Lord. It takes a lot of courage to leave a relationship and start over alone. I had to ask God to help me because I wasn't strong enough to do it on my own. Asking for His help and guidance is one of the best things you can do. He will answer you and help you. He may not do it in the way you expect, but trust Him, it is all working out for your good. As far as family, if you aren't able to completely get them out your life, just create boundaries. For example, set a time for how long you visit or stay on the phone and have an exit strategy to guard you heart.

The Root of Rejection and Abandonment

Let's go a little deeper. The reason why I would get depressed over the lack of a romantic relationship was not only abandonment from my father leaving but also a root of rejection from not receiving the love I needed from my mother. I don't think it was intentional hurt from either of them. As an adult, I've done the work to understand that but my inner child was still deeply wounded by it. I read a book called the 5 languages Of Love, this is where l discovered my love language was words of affirmation. My father tried to affirm me but I wouldn't listen because I hated him. My mom rarely did, I don't think she knew to. Maybe because she was dealing with the aftermath of a divorce, having to work 2 jobs to take care of 4 children with little to no help from my father. So the fact that she worked two jobs to support us and chose to keep us shows that she did love me. It's just that she didn't give me the love that I needed which was affirmation. This caused intense self hatred and mountains of insecurity and never feeling good enough. Whether the lack of love was intentional or not, a deep root of rejection is formed when we don't receive the love we need from a parent or both parents. We then form negative beliefs about ourselves. We also start to go to desperate measures just to feel loved. This can also come from any type of abuse as a child whether it's sexual, verbal or physical or extreme neglect or abandonment such as being placed in foster care or the like. This root of rejection runs deep. It's affects every relationship you're in. It causes you to put extra pressure on every relationship whether romantic or platonic. We expect more and when we don't get it we retaliate. We always end up in the wrong relationship or stay in the relationship years too long because that deep need for love is never full.

It's important to acknowledge our past and accept what happened and forgive. It's easy to place blame and say my father or mother did this or didn't do that or saying I grew up without my father so this is why I'm still like this. They were responsible for how your life began but the great thing is that now the responsibility is all yours. Now you have the opportunity to really change your life. You can take ownership of your hurt and heal it. And you don't have to do it alone. God is with you every step of the way. You have to physically and mentally disconnect from expectation of that person ever being able to fill your voids. This is challenging if the parent, or loved one is still in your life. It's like a sore that never heals and everytime you expect from that person you get hurt all over again. I would read Psalms 27:10 over and over day end and day out. "Although my mother and father have forsaken, yet the Lord will take me up and adopt me as his child". This coupled with Psalms 62:5, "My soul waits only upon God and silently submit to him, for my hope and expectation are from Him". This is the exact food your spirit and soul needs to overcome any root of rejection. This will help you understand that people can't give you what they don't have. Only God can fill voids. When you put your expectation back on Him, He will send the people He wants to be in your life For example, if you don't have a mother or father He will send a mentor that will show you His love and help you on your journey. Just ask Him and trust that He will do it. In the meantime, you become your biggest encourager. He has given you all the power and authority to do this. Just speak His Word over your life every chance you get.

CHAPTER 3
YOU CAN RUN
BUT YOU CAN'T HIDE

We've all had dark times that we don't look forward to. If you've ever dealt with depression you know when that trigger happens. You're like, Oh no not again, how long will this last. This is where you began to think, Is this my life? Am I always gonna be like this? Is there anything I can do? I don't want to be in the dark my whole life. You began to fear the dark, accept the fear of the dark, and live every day or most days in the dark, or you run from it. I mean you have happy moments, like a great career move or you get into a happy relationship or so you thought, but its short-lived because somehow that dark seems to creep up and overshadow your light.

Sometimes we may think that changing our external circumstances will dismiss the darkness but that is furthest from the truth. I finally got the courage to leave my hometown of Atlanta and move to the big city of New York. Living in NY on the outside looked like "girl you made it" but on the inside was a breeding ground for my dark side to haunt me every night. I didn't move to New York specifically to run from my darkness, but I did think because I was in a new state with a new start that it would help, but it was a temporary solution. Also, going from relationship to relationship without really doing the inner work will continue to leave you heartbroken and distressed. If you don't change from the inside out you'll end up in a different state with a different mate but the same old dark volcano waiting to erupt in your life. So, instead of running from your darkness or settling for a quick fix, be brave enough to look it right in the face so you can be free and live the life you truly deserve.

What's your dark side? Depression? Anxiety? Alcoholism? Fear of not being loved? Abandonment Issues? Cutting? Hitting yourself or others? Uncontrollable anger? Excessive worrying, bitterness, rage, paranoia, unforgiveness, as in you hold a grudge forever? The feeling of you're not enough? Fear of not finding your soulmate? Fear of being cheated on if you happen to find your mate? Insecurity? Guilt or shame from things of your past? Are you allowing it to control your life, your thoughts? Where you live, who you date? How you show up in relationships? Or how you show up in life daily? Is it controlling your sleep or lack of sleep? I've shared a snippet of my dark and I'm sure you can relate. Well, whatever it is, enough is enough, right? I know you're tired of living in the dark, secretly hurting and feeling there's no way out. I'm here to tell you there is a way out. You don't have to fear the dark, accept the fear of the dark, or live in the dark another day. There is a light at the end of the tunnel and it includes you being genuinely happy and free. I'm here to show you to the light.

Take Ownership

I took ownership of the state of my mental health in my mid 20's when I realized that I had more bouts with depression that I wanted to admit. Taking ownership requires you to stop hiding and denying your dark and making a decision to face it. Then taking the necessary action to get help. This is when I did a lot of research online to find out exactly what depression was and how to cope with it. It's important not to label yourself and settle in it by just saying I'm depressed, I have anxiety, I have PTSD...and not committing to the Action of Change. This is not the time for a pity party. It's your chance to gird yourself with inner strength and make the decision to push through no matter what. This is why getting a vision is so necessary. When you get weak and discouraged you focus on the end result. You get a mental picture of you being happy, healthy, whole and free, and you hold onto that picture until the vision you see on the inside is more real than what you see on the outside. We'll discuss Vision later on in the book.

CHAPTER 4
WHOLENESS SPIRIT, SOUL, AND BODY

Growing up in an African-American family that did not have a lot of money and also in a Christian African-American family, there were certain things we did and did not do. First, we didn't have insurance so we never went to the doctor. We were definitely taught to pray about everything. We were never taught to talk about our problems with a therapist. That was only for crazy people. Through my journey I realized this was not a balanced way of living and looking at health. Prayer has its place, but we also live in a physical world. And faith without works is dead. So, after praying, pray, that God may lead you to a therapist to help sort out things you could not fix on your own. In church we talk a lot about the spirit and the flesh. But, rarely do we discuss mental health. I have heard some say that the Bible doesn't talk a lot about mental health. I think pastors don't talk a lot about mental health because they don't fully understand it. But, the Bible does talk about mental health when it talks about the soul and the mind.

3 John 2 states, *"I wish above all things that you prosper and be in good health even as your soul prospers."* This is one of many scriptures that talk about the soul and even with this scripture we relate it a lot to money but God wants us to prosper in our mind, thoughts feelings and emotions which is our soul, because whatever you think about the most is what you will bring about in your life.

2 Tim 1:7 states, *"God has not given us a spirit of fear but of power love and a sound mind."* God has given you the power to have a sound mind. Speaking the word of God consistently out your mouth until you believe it will give you a sound mind and this is how you have a prosperous soul instead of a soul filled with darkness.

2 Cor 10:5 states, *"The weapons of this warfare are not carnal but mighty through God to the pulling down of strong holds. Casting down every imagination and every high thing that exalts itself against the word of God, and bringing every thought into captivity to the obedience of Christ."*

Depression is a stronghold of lies that were embedded in you as a child. The lie that you are worthless, that you are not enough; the lie that you are unloved or unwanted or ugly. The lie that you are your experiences and you will always be this way. Depress means to push down, to lose hope, and that's exactly what these thoughts are doing to you; weighing you down and causing you to lose hope day after day. The only way for you to be free is to bring those negative thoughts back to the obedience of Christ who has already set you free. You do this by speaking life every time a negative thought comes, instead of believing the lie or allowing it to just linger. Speak life over it every time.

The only way we can truly win in life is by understanding that we are spirit, we have a soul, and we live in a physical body. And the only way we win is by equally nurturing each part. Having the right food for your spirit, nurturing your soul with the proper tools, and nurturing your physical body. We are used to feeding our body first because that's what we see every day. But, if we can develop a routine where we focus more on our spirit and soul, this is where we truly can be free in our mind, and allow the light of love and understanding into the dark place of our mind and truly be free. Well, how do we change all this? How do we get over the hurt? We must expose the dark, confront the fear, and walk in the newness of life that we deserve.

CHAPTER 5
EXPOSING THE DARK

What happens in the dark will eventually come to the light, right? Not exactly, and not always in the way you want. You can go for years having a secret dark side that no one knows of. The secret of excessive negative thought patterns or holding onto your past and allowing it to control your future. We have to expose the dark to be free from it. The longer it stays a secret it can continue to haunt you, torment you, and rob you of the freedom of being truly happy and whole. If you don't expose it, it will ooze out in other ways that's harmful to you and others. What did I do to get free from the dark? There wasn't one thing I did to get free; it was a bunch of things. And to be honest it took years of research and trial and error to finally get it right. And you can be free too by doing the same things. After I attempted suicide, I realized a few things. One was I didn't want to die, I just wanted the pain to stop. Secondly, I was more hurt than I thought. The pain of the break up triggered a deeper pain that I didn't even know I had. Thirdly, mental health is real. Just praying was not enough, I had to follow up with corresponding actions to really experience true freedom and live in the light.

Understand that the darkness is mostly in your mind. In order for you to be free in your mind your spirit must be connected to God first. That is the foundation you build everything on. You are not your mind or body. They are a part of you but ultimately you are a spirit. So, you have to feed and nurture your spirit first every day with the Word of God. The Word of God in your mind and on your mouth makes you powerful. I will elaborate on this more later.

It's imperative for you to change your foundation. It was involuntarily made from hurt, pain, neglect, disappointment, shame, anger, and betrayal. You have to voluntarily rid your life of all of that by exposing the dark and uprooting the negative thought patterns and beliefs and by retraining your mind.

1. **Expose-** Exposing the dark with love by shedding light on our earliest childhood wounds to allow healing. You can do this just by acknowledging they are there and taking full responsibility for where you are and being open to get help. I initially did this by asking my inner spirit and it showed me my childhood wounds. I then went to a therapist to help expose and uproot them.

2. **Uproot-** Think of uprooting as pulling out the weeds from the root in a garden. You must uproot negative beliefs and thoughts patterns. One way is healing the inner child, which involves changing negative belief patterns. I sought out a therapist to help me do this. This process takes time and patience and understanding. This is why I recommend a therapist because there may be a

lot of layers to uncover and its best not to do this alone. This is what's not taught in church, so I had to step outside of my comfort zone to do something different to get something different. My therapist showed me tools and techniques on how to go back and talk to my inner child and tell her she was enough and speak life into her. This was powerful and freeing at the same time. You can start by writing a letter to your inner child or imagining yourself talking to your inner child like she/he was a child sitting right next to you. We are typically gentle and loving when talking to a child, so you must be the same way when communicating with him/ her. But that is only the tip of the iceberg. My strong suggestion is to seek therapy.

3. **Retrain**- It's not what you know, it's what you believe. And most of your beliefs were formed as a child. So, you have to get relentless in retraining your subconscious mind. You are not your experiences, you are a new creature in Christ. You become new by meditation, reading, speaking and listening to the Word, and other positive messages day and night and even throughout the night.

In order to fully execute all of these tools, you need a plan. You need an intentional growth plan or intentional healing plan. A plan that nurtures your spirit, soul, and body...equally.

CHAPTER 6
INTENTIONAL HEALING PLAN

Spirit Knowledge

God is Spirit and Triune Being. He is made up of God the Father, God the Son, and God the Holy Ghost. One cannot exist without the other. He is a spirit, soul and body. He made us like Him, a trinity being. So, we are a spirit, we have a soul, and live in a physical body. You're more than just a physical body. You are actually not the body that you can see and touch. Your spirit is who you are, and your soul is your mind, will, and emotions, and your body holds them both until you leave the earth.

Understanding that you're a trinity being will help you better understand that you have to be nurtured in each part of "you" to truly live freely. You have to intentionally nurture your spirit, your soul, and your body. We're used to taking care of our physical bodies. We have been conditioned to take care of our physical bodies first, but now we have to recondition ourselves to nurture our spirit and soul as well.

Your spirit is what connects you to God your Creator. It's also how you communicate with God, through your inner spirit, also known as the Holy Spirit living on the inside of you. Your physical body needs food and water and it needs to be nurtured and cared for. We do that by eating the right food, drinking water, taking vitamins, getting rest, exercise, etc. Your spirit needs food. When you don't feed your physical body you get weak. If you've never fed or have stopped feeding your spirit it's gonna be weak and empty. Depression, fear, anxiety, negative self-talk and most of our dark side are symptoms of an empty spirit and wounded soul. Your spirit and soul desperately needs food to quicken it back to life. The best food for you spirit is faith in God and expressing that through worship and intimacy with Him.

Soul Knowledge

Your soul is your mind, will and emotions, your thoughts and feelings. The gates to your soul are your imagination, conscience, memory, reason and affection. It's either full of positive or negative memories. Most have a combination of both negative and positive and whatever is the strongest will control how you think, feel, and respond in situations throughout your life.

Your mind has two parts--a conscious mind and subconscious mind. Your conscious mind is like a gardener; it controls what is sown in your subconscious mind. Your subconscious mind is like a memory bank that stores everything that has ever happened to you. It can store and retrieve data. It's no respect of data, it will store the positive and negative, the great memories as well as the traumatic ones. It's also like fertile ground--whatever is sown in it throughout the years is what it will grow and manifest in your life. Think of your subconscious mind as fertile soil that will grow any seed you plant in it. Well, seeds have been sown in this fertile ground since you were born. Over the years you've formed thought patterns, good and bad. For example, I'm not enough was possibly formed from continuous neglect from a parent or whatever. Money is hard to get was possibly formed from being poor as a child. My fear of abandonment was formed from my father leaving twice, my parents divorcing twice. This was sown at a very young age and it just grew throughout the years. You will always reap what you sow in your mind, consciously or subconsciously. Your thoughts play a major role in planting also. What you think about on a consistent basis is planted in your mind and is what will harvest and grow in your life. The subconscious will either grow flowers or weeds depending on what was planted by your thoughts and thought patterns. It will manifest success or failure. Everything from the time you were born up until now have programmed your subconscious mind. The broken relationship I was in, triggered what was already in the back of my mind the whole time. The fear of getting hurt, the fear of being left or abandoned, the fear of being cheated on. And that subconscious fear is what drew me to that relationship anyway. Wow, deep right? But, instead of beating myself up, running away from the pain of heartbreak or being ashamed and afraid of the dark, I had to intentionally allow love and positive light in to heal every part of my soul. You couldn't control what happened to you as a child. But, you can make a conscience decision to implement techniques to reprogram your sub-conscious mind.

The Power of Love

The light that your darkness needs is love. Unconditional love and unconditional acceptance of yourself. What is love? Love is patient and kind, it doesn't keep a record of wrong. It always hopes and always believes the best of every person, especially and most importantly believes the best of YOU. In order for you to help your dark side, you must be kind to it. We spent most of our lives beating ourselves up for wrong decisions and mistakes and not showing unconditional love and unconditional acceptance to ourselves. Love is powerful. And ultimately our dark side is a part of us and we must embrace it and love it fearlessly. That's exactly what it needs to heal. We can expose our childhood wounds but we must do it in a kind and gentle way. There is no fear in love. Perfect love drives out fear. This unconditional love will not only drive out your fear of your dark side but it will heal it and perfect it. This takes time and patience and it's a process, but if you make a decision to stay committed to the process you will come out whole, complete, and genuinely happy. I've heard it said if you heal the inner child you heal the soul and it's time for you to heal, love, and embrace YOU--every part of you, darkness and all. It's time for you to be intentional about nurturing your whole being, spirit, soul, and body. Because whatever you nurture will grow.

There are seven tools I want to share with you on how to nurture your spirit, soul, and body. They will serve as your Intentional Healing Plan. The great thing about the tools is they are proven and will help get you on a sure path to success. Even if you don't have a dark side, but you just want to ensure continuous growth in the right direction, these techniques will guide you down the right path of wholeness peace, self-love and genuine success. And RESULTS! So are you ready? It's time to go deep!

CHAPTER 7
GO DEEP

Cultivate an intimate relationship with God. One of the most important decisions I had to make was to get serious about healing my spirit. Your spirit is your connection to God. And I realized, every answer I needed, was already inside of me. I just needed to get quiet to connect to spirit and heal the wounds that were there. And the only thing that can truly heal wounds in your heart, soul and spirit, is an intimate, up close and personal relationship with God your Creator. It's the exact nourishment your spirit needs to grow and heal. He is Love, and knows exactly how to love you unconditionally and can teach you how to love yourself too. After all, He made you and loves you so much. He wants to be your friend and live on the inside of you. He wants to talk with you and help uncover your dark side in a loving way that you can grow and heal from. A relationship with God is just communication with Him. An intimate relationship with God is constant communication with Him. Opening up and sharing with Him your deepest darkest thoughts, memories and fears. Talking to God consistently and allowing Him to speak back to you through His Word, your inner voice, through people, a positive message or even a billboard. I feel like I've always had a connection to God but I didn't really know it. I talked to Him most of my life. It started off with me just asking, why am I here? Asking Him for help. And even when I would ask Him not to wake me up the next morning. He heard it all and was there to help and comfort me. God isn't looking for perfection, He just wants a connection with you. He's not mad at you and He's not somewhere waiting to zap you for all the bad things you've done. He longs to be your friend and He wants to talk to you and help you navigate through life. He not only created you but He created you to win and triumph over your enemies. But, we can't win if we don't talk to Him. He wants you to win, and he never meant for you to deal with your darkness alone. He is the one who can lead you to the light and He is the light. Most of the world loves IPhones, and the other half loves Androids. Imagine you being best friends with Steve Jobs before he died and he was able to share with you all the secrets of the IPhone and why he created it and how special and unique it is. What a privilege that would have been. Well, the one who created you wants to sit down and talk to you and tell you all His secrets; why He created you and how special and unique you are, and how loved you are. How there is purpose in your pain and power waiting to be released in your darkness.

During my senior year of high school, I was a ball of uncontrollable hurt and anger. I had gotten into five fights with multiple girls. Finally, my mom told me, you're gonna have to do something different because what you're doing and who you're doing it with is not working. I didn't know exactly what to do, but the church I attended would always take a fast at the beginning of the year, so I decided to use this as an opportunity to try and change. The change I tried a few months before hadn't worked. I tried to just stop cussing and fighting which resulted in another fight because at that time the B word was considered a fighting word. And usually before you would get the word out your mouth, I would have knocked you in the face. But, this time I waited, thinking I had changed but by the 3rd time of her calling me the B word... well, you can only imagine how that ended. I was really hoping this fast would do better than what I tried to do before. So, here's what I did. I got up an hour before it was time for me to get ready for work. I played worship and praise music and I thanked God for waking me up and asked Him to help me. I got out a notebook and I wrote down everything that I thought was wrong with me at that time. Things like anger, lust, unforgiveness, disrespectful to my parents, etc. Then I opened the Bible, went to the back and found scriptures on each one, and wrote the scriptures down. I then turned the scriptures into personal affirmations, or what my church called confessions at that time. I began to say the confessions out loud. For example. I didn't feel complete or whole. I looked up the word complete and found the scripture Col 2:10 that said *"I am complete in Jesus who is the head of all principalities and power."* I didn't know what a principality was at that moment but I knew I wanted to be complete, so I read it and said it aloud three times a day. I learned that when you fast, you give up certain things and replace it with prayer and time with God. My church would fast from certain foods and meat. Since I was already super thin, I decided to keep meat but just eat baked fish or chicken. I decided to give up my phone and talking to my boyfriend and friends at that time. This was the equivalent of giving up Social Media today. We fasted for 30 days, January 1-30. I was used to talking to my boyfriend and friends in my free time but since I couldn't talk to them, I filled that time with saying my confessions and listening to a Word message three times a day. I did this in the morning before work, on my lunch break, and when I got home from work. I also attended church at least three times a week, which was Sunday, Wednesday and Fridays. I didn't just attend church, I brought a notebook and took notes and studied them later. To my surprise, I started to become happier. I felt lighter and overall joyful. The real change for me was forgiveness. See, I hated my dad. Hate is a strong word, but I can honestly say I hated him. I didn't want to be in the same room with him. I hated going to his house on weekends after my parent's divorce. I have even hit my dad… why he didn't hit me back only the Lawd knows. But yea, I hated him with a passion. I didn't know any other emotion to feel toward him but hate. I had so much hurt, anger, and bitterness on the inside of me.

So, when I started to forgive my dad and love him, I actually wanted to be in the same room as him. And hug him.

I knew then that there was something phenomenal about spending intimate time with God. Forgiveness is not something I had planned on doing. I wasn't even thinking that far down the line. So, when my heart softened toward my dad without me asking or even wanting it to, God in that moment became more real to me than ever before. I changed in so many ways. The presence of God gave me what I wanted and things I didn't even know I needed. And everyone noticed. I wasn't "mean" Tina anymore. God, the Creator of the universe, became my friend. He used His Word to heal me, and love me, and restore me back to life. I was alive but this is the first time I felt like I was living. I felt free, like a new person. I was no longer controlled by anger. I even called most of the girls I fought and apologized for my actions. WHAT? Me? I couldn't believe it. This intimate time with God gave me confidence, wholeness, and peace of mind. Something I had never felt before.

From Pain to Purpose

After taking time to nurture and strengthen my spirit and love for myself, I was so excited I wanted to share my change with other young girls my age. This is when God turned my pain into purpose. See, I had always had problems with girls not liking me, being jealous or whatever. I would try to be nice and when that didn't work, I would beat them up. It wasn't that hard because I was already angry from wounds from early childhood. But, instead of me wanting to fight physically, I realized that I could fight God's way, with love, forgiveness, and kindness. So, at 18 years old I founded a non-profit organization for girls called FAVOR which stood for Flourishing Flowers Ardouring Virtue and Obtaining Righteousness. I began having sleepovers at my home once a month. We would eat pizza and talk about how to apply God's Word to our lives and relationships at our age. It was impactful and life changing and fun. It started with seven or eight girls and grew to 150 young teens in my mom's garage. Crazy right? This was a real live example of turning pain into purpose, all because of an intimate relationship with God.

Fill Up

Your natural body needs food and if it doesn't get it you won't survive. Time with God is the food your spirit needs to survive, and not only survive, but thrive. He loves you, and He is for you. He wants you to succeed in all areas of your life. His love is not like human love. It doesn't hurt. He will show you patience and kindness, and show you how to be patient and kind to others and yourself.

For a while I was holding back and I didn't really know how to fully receive His love. It was even hard to look at Him as my Friend and Father because I had been betrayed by so many people, including my father, and so-called friends and family. Even though my first experience with love was broken He showed me a type of love a man or human could never live up to and a love that could never be taken away. So, if you're struggling with love, a lack of it, and even not knowing how to love yourself, model after His love and trust me you will never be disappointed.

When I first started developing my own relationship with God, I used to just get up and pray in the bed. But, after years of doing that it just got old and I got lazy. And to be honest, after going through so much stuff in life, I needed something more. I actually saw this on the movie called WAR ROOM, so I decided to try it for myself. I had a room in my home that was supposed to be an office but it was filled with junk and we never used it, so it was more like a storage room. I pushed and pushed and pushed every day to get it cleaned out. I ordered a couple of items online to make it look like a nice office with cute things that I loved. Over on the side, I placed some nice pillows and candles, and I posted positive things on the wall. It was very inviting and it made me feel excited, which also made me happy about getting back into the presence of God.

So, I set a time each morning to get up and go downstairs, turn on the lights and music and sit there. That's all it was initially. I read a scripture; I read a devotion; but I didn't feel anything. I know you're not supposed to always feel something, but I really wanted to. I had a lot of internal mess that I needed to get out. I went down each day in faith and expectation. I also kept a journal each day and tried to write down anything positive I felt. I think within like a month's time something finally broke and I began to feel the presence of God. I began to feel him gently touch my heart; I began to cry. I began to break. It wasn't God that wasn't there, I wasn't there. I was so full of hurt and pain, I was just hard as a rock. He had to break me so I could feel Him and that's when my heart begin to soften toward Him and toward life. I began to feel joy and peace again.

I don't want to make spending time with God any more complicated than it already may sound, so here are a few steps that will help out with that.

1. **Wake up and Win!**

   Set your alarm to get up 20-30 minutes or more before its time to actually get up and get dressed for work.

2. **Create Space!**

   Prepare a quiet place to meet daily. A place with no distractions. It can be a closet, an area in your room, or the hallway. Make it inviting, with pillows, candles, and maybe a nice small picture or blanket.

3. **Strap Up!**

   Bring a notebook, Bible and music. The great thing about technology is all this can be done on your phone or tablet. You can play music on YouTube, write in your notes, and download the Bible App. I love the Bible app. It has a variety of translations and devotions that you can read every day. You can set reminders too. I prefer to write in an actual journal, to keep all my notes in one place, but I have jotted down things in my phone also. There was a time when the first thing I did when I woke up was pray. Well, since social media, it easily turned into going straight to Facebook or Instagram. But, I realized that was part of the reason I was so empty. I was filling my head with mess every morning and perpetuating the emptiness on the inside. I literally had to remove the apps from my phone for 30 days, so that when I looked for it, it wasn't there and I reconditioned myself to go straight to my Bible app.

4. **Set the Mood!**

Set the atmosphere with soft music, preferably worship and praise music. I love Hillsong, Kari Jobe, Tasha Cobbs, and Tye Tribbett. I love the songs Oceans & Fill me Up. I would play these songs over and over on repeat.

5. **Get Inspired!**

Read the Bible, 1-3 Scriptures. Some of my favorites are Psalms 23, 62, 63 and 84. I love reading Psalms because it talks a lot about the soul and that's exactly where we need the healing. Find 1 or 2 scriptures that work for you and read them every day. The Bible can seem big and overwhelming. Just focus on a few scriptures that give you strength.

Read a Devotional each morning. They even have

scriptures after the devotional that you may want to read. Once again the Bible App has great devotionals, but I also read Jesus Calling, by Sarah Young. I love this book. It's one of my favorites. I own the actual book but it's also available as an App too.

6. **Give thanks!**

Say Thank You Lord for this beautiful day. Thank you Lord for my life health and strength. Thank you Lord for meeting me here today. Just give thanks for everything you can think of.

7. **Ask!**

Ask Him for a hunger and thirst for His Word and presence. Ask Him for strength and to help you to trust Him. Ask Him for an awareness of His presence and for wisdom, or for whatever you need. And then thank Him. You only have to ask once and then thank Him after that.

8. **Real talk**

Now just talk to Him. Say whatever is on your heart and be totally honest. I would say things like, God I'm so mad right now. I can't believe I got myself into this again. God, I need you, help me. I would talk to Him like He was my friend. I have even cussed when talking to Him. Not at Him, but if I was angry that is what would come out. He is not there to judge you, but love you. And He will love the Hell out of you! I recommend you try talking to Him throughout the day too.

9. Get Quiet.

Get quiet and expect to hear from Him. Sometimes you'll hear something right then, or you may hear something later in the day. If you feel you heard something write it down, even if it's one word. If not, don't get discouraged. He will speak eventually through your inner spirit. There were times I was so depressed and I didn't have the energy to do any of this. I could only lay there and cry. That's ok, He is still there. Find a good Word message and just listen to it over and over and just lay and receive. He got you.

Develop a habit of spending time with God first thing in the morning before you open social media and before bed. Then add it throughout the day, in the shower, or on the way to work. You'll get so addicted. Everything you need is in His presence. This will bring so much unexplainable joy to your life. You'll begin to recognize His voice or a gentle nudge in the right direction or a hunch to not go a particular way. Watch the light of His unconditional love heal your darkness. Stay close to Him long enough for Him to heal you, fill you, until you overflow with goodness, love and joy.

CHAPTER 8
GET YO LIFE!

So, let's recap. The first step to healing is an intimate relationship with God that will feed and nurture your spirit. But, the next step was hugely powerful for me as well: affirmations. Affirmations are powerful medicine for your soul and the ultimate way to have a love relationship with yourself. And one of the vital ways to heal the soul and retrain your subconscious mind. It's time for you to start loving you! After I attempted suicide, I talked to God and asked Him how did I have a relationship with you and get to the point where I wanted to take my life and actually tried. And to my surprise He spoke back through my spirit and said "you did not use your weapon." My weapon? You did not use your weapon to fight the enemy. Your weapon is your mouth and even more the Word of God in your mouth. God created you like Him, a speaking spirit. Your life and your death is in the power of your tongue. And the same way He spoke light in the midst of darkness, you have the power to speak light in your dark life. And if you don't use your weapon and speak life you will forever be poisoned by your darkness instead of empowered by it.

Having a relationship with God gives you power and authority. Speaking the Word and affirmations out of your mouth allows you to use your power and authority. God created you to fight; He created you to be a warrior and to win, and the only way you win is by using the right weapon and using it consistently. Even though you may not want to fight you were created to fight.

In my life I fought, but I fought wrong and I used the wrong weapons. My fist and foul language were not the right weapons. You can't use physical weapons to solve or win a spiritual war and problem. When your soul is under attack, being tormented by darkness, you have make a decision to intentionally speak life only. You have to get relentless and speak life only multiple times a day. When you're sick in your physical body and you go to the doctor he will prescribe you medicine and he'll tell you to take it three times a day, and even if you start to feel better don't stop taking it. It's the same way with your soul; it is sick and you have to speak life which is your medicine at least three times a day, and even if you start to feel better you don't stop and this is how you bring light in your darkness.

We have to be very careful with our words, choosing to speak only those which work toward our benefit and cultivate our highest good. Affirmations help purify our thoughts and restructure the brain. We can truly begin to think only good, healthy, happy, and whole thoughts about ourselves and manifest only the best in our life. The word affirmation comes from the Latin word affirmare, originally meaning "to make steady, strengthen." Affirmations strengthen us from the inside out. When we verbally affirm ourselves constantly we are instantly empowered and release an assurance that what we see is temporary and our best life is here now. Affirmations are proven methods of self-love and self-improvement because of their ability to reprogram our mind. Just like exercise releases endorphins to help us feel better, affirmations are a brain exercise that releases feel good energy to help improve our state of mind and change our negative thought patterns. This is one of the most effective ways to GET YO LIFE! To overcome fear, anger and rewrite your future. I tried to take my life because I didn't love me. I didn't see any value in my life. Now, I speak valuable things to myself. If you want a better life, Speak it! If you constantly say you can't, you won't. But, if you say you can you will eventually believe you can and you will. Just think about every negative thing that has been said over your life since you were born; this is exactly what's in your subconscious mind and this is what's holding you back in the darkness and preventing you from coming to the real light. This is the best opportunity for you to speak life and become your best cheerleader and reprogram every negative thing that was said about you into something brilliant and powerful. This is your chance to create the life of your dreams. This is the best way to believe in yourself. You don't get what you want in life, you get what you believe. This will change your belief. You can let go of all the negative thoughts and images that control your subconscious mind and replace them with new thoughts and images that are positive and stated in the present tense. Use your voice to win! There is power in the statement "I am." God said "I Am That I Am." And He gave you that same authority. Pause...don't you like that word authority? It means the power or right to give orders. You have been given the power and right to order darkness right out of your life and bring in the light. When negative thoughts fill your mind, don't let them sit there. Evict them out of your mind right then and there with the power of I am.

The Message In Your Pain

When you experience pain your mind gives it a message. It's the thought behind the pain that can be worse than the pain. It could be telling you that you're worthless, you aren't worthy of love, that something is wrong with you that can't be fixed. You're unlovable. God doesn't love you, God is mad at you. You're ugly, and the thoughts go on and on. This is why you stay depressed for so long. Because of the strongholds in your mind. They're all lies. This is why retraining your subconscious mind is so vital. So you can change the message. It's time for you to speak to your pain, tell it it's temporary and the joy of the Lord is forever. Speak to it and tell it you are loved. You are worthy of love. God loves you and He is not mad at you. You are fearfully and wonderfully made by God. He has a plan and a purpose for your life. And this pain will work out for your good! Change the message in your pain so you can believe the best of yourself and others.

Here's how!

1. Write down a list of affirmations. I would say at least 10. For example:

   I am powerful. I am resilient. I am strong. I am wise. I am so creative. I am brilliant. I am free.

2. Now write down affirmations about what you want specifically in the present tense.

   Two examples would be:

   I am joyfully walking out my purpose and living my best life daily.

   I am so happy and grateful that I am enjoying a wonderful relationship with my soul mate.

3. Say them at least once a day. If you need healing I would suggest 3x a day and as needed.

4. Say them with excitement. If you're healing you may have to grow to this. But say them with excitement as if it has already happened.

5. Make a list of all the negative beliefs and lies in your head. For example. I'm not enough. I'm weak. I can't take this. And say the opposite. I am enough. I am strong. I am resilient. Then throw that negative list away and keep the positive.

6. Turn scripture into affirmations.

Ex: Col 2:10 *"I am complete in Jesus who is the head of all principality and power."*

Psalms 34: *"I sought you Lord and I am healed and delivered me out of all my fears. I look to you and I am enlightened and my face is not ashamed. I thank you Lord that you're near me and you've healed my broken heart and I am delivered out of all my afflictions."*

Psalms 23: *I thank you Lord that you refresh and restore my soul. That even though I walk through the valley of the shadow of death. You are always with me and protect me. You anoint my head with oil, my cup runs over. And your goodness and mercy will always follow me and overtake me forever.*

I have said affirmations on and off for over 20 years. They have truly been my medicine and vitamins in the morning. And it has brought tremendous change in my life as well as helped me believe in myself and grow in confidence and self-love. I learned later in life that the more excited you are when you say them, the more your mind receives it as true. So, now I make sure I say them with excitement and assurance as if it's already in my life and what I'm saying has already come to pass. It's easy, it's highly effective, and also proven to lower stress levels. If you continue to say what is or what you don't want you'll continue to get just that. Make a decision today to speak life only. I am! I am! I am!

Write down 10 affirmations you are choosing to say over your life now.

1. _____

_____

2. _____

_____

3. _____

_____

4. _____

_____

5. _____

_____

6. _____

_____

7. _____

_____

8. _____

_____

9. _____

_____

10. _____

_____

CHAPTER 9
LET GO

You have to forgive and let go. If you truly want to turn your pain from poison to power, forgiveness is so vital. I've heard it said that forgiveness is an event and a process. It's a decision you make that day, and then you have to choose to continue to forgive daily. Forgiveness is not always easy, and it does not condone, approve, excuse or minimize what was done to you. Forgiving is a choice, it's not forgetting or giving them permission to hurt you again. It's a decision not to retaliate, take revenge or hold resentment. It takes time but making this decision benefits you more than the person that needs forgiving. Unforgiveness is like you drinking poison and hoping the other person dies. You also have to let go of every negative emotion that is trying to poison you. Anger, rage, resentment, bitterness, worry, fear. Sometimes we hold on to these emotions because it's like a barrier to protect us from ever getting hurt by them or anyone else. If you experienced deep trauma, especially in childhood, some of these wounds may be painful to bring up and let go of. And some of them you may not know is there but it's subconsciously affecting your daily life and decisions. You have to expose the hurt and pain in order to truly heal from it. You can do this in a couple ways. Just find what works for you and do it.

HOW TO FORGIVE

1. **Acknowledge!**

   Acknowledge the exact incident that happened and exactly how you felt about it.

2. **What's the lesson?**

   What lessons can you learn from the incident about yourself and life? What good can you take away from it? And how did you grow from it?

3. **Pray for them.**

   When you pray for the person that hurt you, you are wishing them well. This may be hard in the beginning. But, this will help release the anger and soften your heart. You will begin to see them as a flawed human and understand that hurt people hurt people. So pray that their hurt is healed also. This pushes you toward healing and away from the unhealthy attachment to them.

4. **Just Do It!**

   Forgiveness is a choice, so say often I choose to forgive. I forgive you. There is power in the spoken word.

HOW TO LET GO

1. Ask God!

One way is just asking God, and eventually your inner spirit will reveal it. I remember years ago, I used to spaz out when the threat of my boyfriend leaving would happen. I honestly didn't know why. It's not until we broke up and I was really trying to get over the hurt and realized it was a lot harder than I thought. He began to show me the root of my hurt and pain and where it all began. There were specific memories He brought back to me that exposed why I had a lack of trust and abandonment issues. It was a painful process but it was also enlightening and helped me understand myself more. I also asked Him to help me get over my ex and remove the pain and the memory of the break up as if it never happened. With consistent prayer time, saying my affirmations, and listening to positive messages, eventually I was completely over the relationship, no hard feelings and no longing to still be with him. God can heal your broken heart if you let Him. He taught me to trust Him, to fill my voids, and not look for those voids to be filled in wrong relationships. I learned that He is my rock, and strength and my expectation is from Him.

2. **Therapy: It's not a bad word.**

I moved to New York when I was 25. This was a big deal for me. I finally got the courage to step out on my own and pursue my dreams. I left Atlanta, but the hurt and pain of my past followed me. I would have nightmares and wake up crying. I started having flashbacks from my past. Some of the things I didn't consciously remember but clearly they were embedded in me. This is when I decided to go seek professional help. I didn't have insurance to pay for therapy. But, I found a group that had a sliding scale payment plan that I could afford and I put money aside to go. The therapist allowed me to see that I was dealing with PTSD and also gave me tools and strategies to deal with it at that time. I realized I could not do this alone, and yes, God is always with me but there are also professionals that will help you find an answer. Therapy is not a bad word. It's just another way of showing yourself love. Don't be afraid to go talk to someone. Finding a therapist can be challenging because you have to sort through and find one that you connect with but be determined.

3. **Google it!**

There were also times where I did my own research online and ordered books and listened to audible teachings to help. The point is, I did something. I did not allow the lack of insurance or low income stop me from getting to the light. We are conditioned to surf the internet looking for the latest tea, but imagine what would happen if you were to put that energy into finding solutions for yourself. Just google it. Put whatever you're going through in the search engine of Google or even YouTube. Tons of articles and videos will come up. Read, listen and win.

4. **Release Ceremony.** The first time I did a release ceremony, I was at a point where I was dealing with a lot of hurt and brokenness again, and I was filled with anger resentment and sarcasm to go along with it. I knew I needed to release some things, but honestly didn't know how. I had chosen to forgive but I still felt like I was holding onto the after thoughts of what happened and it affected my mood and everything. A life coach friend of mine suggested I do a release ceremony. I didn't know exactly what she meant but she was kind enough to explain it step by step. I loved the idea so much. I knew I had to give it a try. What did I have to lose? I went home and did everything she instructed me to do. Afterward, I immediately felt lighter and freer, like a weight had been lifted off of my shoulders. A release ceremony has been a pivotal part of my healing. It's a powerful technique and it's something I do as often as needed. It's been helpful to myself and to others, in working to release anger, pain and other difficult emotions that can hinder growth and progress.

It is not meant to replace any needed psychological counseling or mental health help that might be needed. If you have mental or emotional challenges that are affecting your ability to function normally, please see a qualified counselor of your choosing to help. This release ceremony is a wonderful addition to combine with therapy and prayer as you take steps toward healing and reclaiming your life. I want to share with you the process of creating your own release ceremony. Here are the steps below. I encourage you to give it a try, and don't be afraid to put your own spin on it too.

Release Ceremony

1. Carve out time where you won't be bothered for a least 1-2 hours.
2. Go to a quiet place like your bedroom floor or closet or wherever it's quiet.
3. Grab 20 or more sheets of paper and a pen or pencil.
4. Write on the top of the page "I Choose to Release. I Choose to let go."
5. Start off with every negative emotion you can think of that you want release and let go. For example, write I choose to release, I choose to let go: hurt, pain, anger, resentment, unforgiveness etc. Just keep writing until you have gotten them all out. If something comes up for you later then write it down. (the first time I did this I had

over 20 emotions to release!)

6. Write down "I choose to forgive. I choose to let go". Next, write all the people you want to forgive. If this is your first time, start from your first memory of hurt and go from there.

7. Write every individual memory and the details of what happened, how it made you feel and everything. After each memory write "I choose to forgive. I choose to let go."

8. Now list each memory where you can offer forgiveness to yourself. After each memory, write, "I choose to forgive I choose to let go."

9. Repeat this process until you feel you have gotten everything out.

10. Write these phrases 10 times each: I forgive I let go, I am free I am whole I am enough. Now at this point you should began to feel lighter. Just keep repeating writing it until you feel peace.

11. Grab all your sheets of paper, and get ready to burn them. If you have a grill outside that would be perfect. If not, tear the paper into small pieces and consider flushing down the toilet (just be mindful of your plumbing). And even with the burning, do it in a safe way. If you choose to burn it, watch the bad memories burn to ashes, Consider playing a song like Andra Day-Rise up; it really helps puts things in perspective.

12. Once everything is burned or flushed, grab a separate sheet of paper and write who you're going to show up as from now on. Write new affirmations, and repeat the ones that stand out to you a few times, For example: I choose to show up whole happy and free. I am new. I am resilient. I am powerful. I am enough. I am kind. I am gentle to myself and others. I'm free. I show up wise strong and brilliant. This is an important step because you are filling the space you created with new and positive things. Keep writing until you feel it's enough and at this point you're done. You will genuinely feel lighter like a huge weight has been lifted from your entire being.

Make your release ceremony your own. Again, this is YOUR healing, so get creative and listen to your heart. I chose to burn my paper because I didn't want anything left over from it. It was very symbolic watching it burn into ashes and I played Audra Day's song "I will rise up" over and over again until all my papers were just ashes. I felt like my spirit was saying I'm giving you beauty for ashes and I loved every minute. Once it was done I went back upstairs and I wrote down everything to describe the new me I was committing to being, and the woman I would be from that point on. It was both a commitment and declaration at the same time. I can honestly say that I felt lighter, brighter, happier, and freer. I saw a change in my mood and I could feel myself more present in my everyday life. So, if you have some contaminating thoughts, emotions, memories, or feelings that you know you need to let go of but you haven't been successful. This may be the best tool for you. If you feel you still have deep rooted issues that are still challenging to let go, again, definitely consider professional counseling and or a life coach. Don't let money or resources stop you. Check with your local church for free or sliding fee scale options.

A Date With Healing

On this page set a date and time you're going to do your Release Ceremony.

Release Ceremony

Date

_____

Time

_____

CHAPTER 10
INVEST!

As you move down the path of healing and wholeness, be aware of everything that you expose yourself to. It matters. Your eyes, ears, and mouth are the gateways to your heart and soul. Take care in what you're watching and reading and listening to; this is key in retraining your subconscious mind

Read positive books only. Read books specifically on what you're going through and positive books that inspire you. There are so many out there. Don't get overwhelmed, you can start with 15 minutes a day. Make it fun and reward yourself after you complete a book. Some people make fun of self-help books, but I look at them as self-love books. Love yourself enough to invest in you; you are so worth it.

Watch inspiring things only. Guard your eye gate relentlessly from the news, movies, TV shows, and social media posts. You don't want to intentionally trigger your dark side, protect it like a baby. You wouldn't let your children watch certain things, or at least I hope you wouldn't. So while you're on this journey of healing, just be careful.

Listen to positive things only...all the time, around the clock if possible. Especially first thing in the morning and before you go to bed. And also throughout the night. A lot of times when you're depressed you don't even have the energy to open your mouth to say anything but lay there.

So, while you lay there make a decision to play positive messages. Find a pastor or preacher or a positive message that you like and play it over and over and over. It's also very important for you to listen throughout the night because this is how you can train retrain your subconscious mind the quickest, because your conscious mind is asleep. We know subconsciously you can have a lot of fear, hurt, anger, and wrong thought patterns. But making a decision to play positive affirmations or a positive message on repeat will change your life. And when you get the energy take notes on the message that you're hearing and this will also help change you from the inside out. Retraining the subconscious mind takes time patience and consistency and a lot of repetition. Depression is a mountain of wrong thought patterns, emotions and feelings. A stronghold, and if you speak to it consistently and add listening to a positive message you will break it down. I've learned that what's written is what's real so when you take the time to write out a message that's really impactful in your life you are also writing it on your subconscious mind. During my lowest times I would just lay there and press play. We have smart phones now so we can play anything we choose at any time. This is perfect because no matter where you are you can make a choice to pour into yourself positive things. I'm an audible.com and YouTube geek. I'm listening to one or both every day and on my off days, all day. I just play positive messages on repeat daily, and especially throughout the night. This habit will definitely transform your life inside and out.

Write down 3 to 5 positive messages and inspiring books and make a decision to start listening and reading today.

_____

_____

_____

_____

_____

_____

_____

_____

_____

_____

_____

_____

_____

_____

CHAPTER 11
GOT VISION?

I made my first vision board in 2007. A vision board is a collage of images, words and anything that helps you visualize who you want to be and the life you want to live. Having a vision brings clarity to your dreams and helps you stay focused when you get sidetracked or stressed. It reminds you of what really matters in your life. You can also consider a dream book, the only major difference is one's a board and one's a book.

I spent the whole year of 2008 looking at my vision board every morning and every night. I had on there marriage, three children, I had a beautiful wedding ring, beautiful dress, a beautiful wedding, and I also had career goals, ministry goals business goals and whatever I felt inspired by. My first desire and also main fear was a love relationship. I was wanting it and afraid of it at the same time. In order to deal with my fear I filled the board with happy couples to retrain my thought pattern of toxic relationships. To be honest, I got very discouraged and at some point I threw it under my bed, frustrated as if it didn't work. The very next year I met my husband and it wasn't until after we got married that I ran across my vision board and a lot of things that we had was on my vision board! The ring, the wedding, and three beautiful children. So, the moral of the story is write the vision and make it plain. Don't give up, it will come to pass. Just as with your affirmations, look at your vision board with excitement as if what you're expecting has already happened. This will make it that much easier to bring things to pass. All that positive mental energy is powerful!

Take some time and print out the new life that you desire. Pictures of you happy, taking trips, a loving family, smiling, laughing, financially free and whole. Look at those pictures every day once or twice a day. What kind of person do you want to be? What do you want to achieve? A vision board is the best way to display your dreams and have easy access to look at daily. You can also create a picture collage on your phone and set it to music and look at it every day.

Write down the new life you want. And on a separate board or book create your new reality!

CHAPTER 12
GIVE THANKS OFTEN!

Gratitude opens the door to so many miracles in your life, quickly. The two best ways to express gratitude is, of course, by saying it and by keeping a gratitude journal. In your gratitude journal write, I'm so happy and grateful that I'm enjoying my new life of wholeness and peace. I'm so happy and grateful that I feel so loved right now, thank you Jesus. I'm so happy and grateful that I'm surrounded by love. I'm so happy and grateful that I'm enjoying healing, happiness, and a great life. This will create an instant energy of joy.

This was one of the best things I could have ever added in my life! I wish I would have done it sooner. I've only been practicing this for about 2 years but my life has drastically changed internally and externally. This may be the most overlooked tool but it's so easy to do and the benefits are endless. It truly opens the door to miracles daily. I'm getting excited just writing about it. Since I have started journaling my gratitude, I've experienced overall better mental and physical health, genuine joy and happiness, an improved relationship with myself and my husband and children. So many blessings like a new house, new car, and unexpected income. Real peace and better relationships overall and so much more. I love it. It's been scientifically proven to do all the results I listed as well. I would suggest writing in your gratitude journal in the morning when you get up and at night before you go to bed. This will help you start your day with joy and expectation to find more things to be grateful for throughout the day. And it's been proven to help you sleep better at night. All I can say is try it; you are guaranteed to love it. You can express gratitude for the past present and future.

For example:

1. Past: I'm so grateful for this wonderful house; it's truly a blessing.

2. Present: Thank you Lord for the wonderful gift of life; I'm so grateful

3. Future: I'm so happy and grateful for the check I received for $1000. This is so awesome, Thank you!

The best part about this is when you write in it as if it's already happened your mind will act as if it already happened and work with God to produce it. Gratitude is also one of the highest expressions of trust in God. You're saying, I already know you've worked this out. Thank you! Understand that when you complain, you remain. When everything in your life is going crazy and you choose to still thank Him in the midst of the craziness, watch how quickly things turn around. Instead of talking about everything that is going wrong and what you don't have, choose to focus on the things you do have and give thanks. Thank you Lord that this is working out for my good! This is also called a sacrifice of praise. I had two friends who both lost their jobs on separate occasions. Both were distraught and I asked them what can you be grateful for right now? I'm telling you one within 24 hours and the other within 48 hours both had new jobs that was a lot better than the jobs they were fired from. Won't He Do It?! Choose to have an attitude of gratitude today.

Write down 5-10 things you're grateful for now!

1. _____

_____

2. _____

_____

3. _____

_____

4. _____

_____

5. _____

_____

6. _____

_____

7. _____

_____

8. _____

_____

9. _____

_____

10. _____

_____

CHAPTER 13
DIET & EXERCISE

Exercise and healthy eating has always been an on and off journey for me. Sometimes, I eat right and don't exercise; other times I exercise and not eat right; and then there are the great times I do both. I've realized that they're both essential to emotional healing. So, I make sure I keep both in my life on some level. The easiest way for me to eat right in a way that's balanced is eating healthy (whole grains, fruits, vegetables, and lean meat) about 5-6 days a week. I'll give myself at least one day a week to have comfort food as a treat. Taking vitamins like omega 3's and B12 are also proven to boost your mood, so I take them regularly. We know endorphins are released when you exercise and that definitely helps depression. There are so many wonderful exercise techniques to explore. Find one that works for you and do it often, preferably 3x a week. I strongly suggest yoga because it also works your mind, but the choice is yours. Finding an exercise partner to be accountable to is great and will increase your chances of staying consistent. I always say make it fun and reward yourself as an incentive to stay disciplined. And on the journey of self-love it's always good to celebrate yourself often.

Medication. I have to be honest I was totally against medication. But it's not until a woman I respected years ago shed light on medication. That it's not the answer but can help aid you and help you on the path to mental health and wholeness. Some really need it and others use it to numb the pain or escape reality. I made a pact with myself in my late 20s that if I ever got severely depressed again I would consider medication. It wasn't until years later that I actually made the step to try a mild medication for depression. I only stayed on it for a short time and I did not allow it to replace the holistic essential tools that I knew would change my life. I allowed it to give me the will to want to do the work that needed to be done. With that being said don't start taking meds to get high and escape your dark side. If you are addicted to the meds you've already been taking, find the courage to get help. You deserve to have a pain-free, drug-free life, and stress-free life the right way. I suggest you do your own research on what medication is being suggested and its side effects. Then do what's BEST for you.

Write down a new exercise and healthy eating habit you'll add to your life this week.

New Exercise:

_____

_____

_____

_____

_____

_____

_____

_____

_____

_____

_____

Healthy Eating Habit:

_____

_____

_____

_____

_____

_____

_____

_____

_____

CHAPTER 14
SUCCESS ROUTINE

I've shared a wealth of knowledge and tools to help you genuinely succeed in life. It's not meant to overwhelm you, but inspire you to take action now. I called this an intentional healing plan, but once you're healed this can become your success routine. After marriage and having children, I began to get overwhelmed and tired from all the extra responsibility. This affected my quiet time in the mornings where I spent time with God, affirmed myself, etc. Life got busier and I got more empty, and when trouble hit it drained me even more. I was desperately trying to get back on track but it seemed like life pushed me further and further away. This is when depression creeped it's way right back in. I knew I had to do something. So, I started listening to messages on YouTube for personal growth and development. I ran across a message from Terri Savelle Foy called 5 Things Successful People Do Before 8am. This message spoke volumes in my life. It was only 9 minutes, but I listened to it over and over. All of a sudden it hit me. I stopped doing the things that made me succeed in life. I just started existing and life began to get the best of me. A few of the tools in the Intentional Growth Plan have been documented as things successful people do daily. The crazy part is I didn't know that. So, I needed to aggressively pick up the habits I had before and even add better habits to them.

Success is found in your daily routine. It's been said if you do something for 21 days straight, you'll drop an old habit and start a new one. I also heard that's been updated to 60-90 days. Either way, make a decision today to commit to your Intentional Healing Plan for 30 days, then repeat that. John Maxwell calls it the Rule of 5. This is where you choose 5 things to commit to every morning for success. Others call it a Success Routine. But, whatever you choose to call it, Just Do it. My 5 things I have to do every morning in order to stay full and attract success are:

1. Quiet time with God. (Step 1, Go Deep)
2. Say Affirmations
3. Visualize and review my goals and dreams
4. Journal my Gratitude
5. Listen to a positive message

Fill Your Cup

This is MY ultimate success routine. What's yours? I now know and understand that I have to do these 5 steps EVERYDAY to keep myself full. When my joy tank is full, depression doesn't stand a chance! However, life gets busy and a few days may go by and I haven't taken time to fill up. I start feeling overwhelmed, low or empty and my thoughts start to get negative, fearful or doubtful. That's when I have to pause and check my gas light. I'll ask myself have you filled up today? Then I'll stop whatever I'm doing and go to a quiet place and take some time and fill myself up by reading a scripture in psalms, saying my affirmations, or if I'm in the car I'll play a positive message. If I'm at work, I take a break and either go to the restroom or car and fill up.

Even something great in your life and can cause you to get overwhelmed and depressed. For example we recently bought a home and it was a major blessing that I'm truly grateful for. However, life naturally got a little out of sync. We had to pack up the old place and move into a new place all while maintaining our normal schedule. Of course that means getting up earlier and staying up later etc. When I felt myself feeling overwhelmed. I paused, took a couple deep breaths and exhaled "Thank you Lord for this blessing. Thank you Lord for this gift, Thank you Thank you Thank you" I would not allow myself to complain not one minute. Immediately, I felt joy fill my spirit.

The point is don't wait for someone to fill your cup. You take the responsibility to check your own gauge and fill your own cup. Only you know when "something isn't right". Just pause and take 5 to 10 minutes to pour back into yourself and you'll feel so much better. Often times we look for people to complete us or fill us. When it doesn't happen we become irritable, critical, short tempered or frustrated. God is the only one that can fill you and complete you. He has empowered YOU to fill YOU. Just do it!

Just Do It!

Write down at least 5 steps you will commit to for 30 days. Be intentional and prepare. Set a date and go for it.

1. _____

_____

2. _____

_____

3. _____

_____

4. _____

_____

5. _____

_____

CHAPTER 15
KEEP CALM
AND CARRY ON

When all else fails, keep calm and carry on. Stay consistent and don't quit. If you get off the mark start again and again and again. This is not a challenge but a lifestyle change. Real change takes time and patience and persistence. When you make a decision to change sometimes things get worse before they get better. But, remember you are powerful. You can do this! Jim Rohn said it best, "Success is neither magical nor mysterious. Success is the natural consequence of consistently applying basic fundamentals". It's not what you do one time but repeatedly over and over that truly changes your life. So don't give up! Consistency is key when you want to see real change and real results. Just set a date sooner than later and go for it and keep going. Change is a journey, not a destination. These are things that I do daily to keep myself full and whole. Initially, when I started this process, I was very empty and sometimes it was hard to do, but I kept going. Slowly, I felt myself getting better, less depressed and happier. Soon after the good life became normal and depression became abnormal. I can't say I don't ever have down days, because I do, but what I can say is that I know exactly what to do when they come.

Called To Greatness

As I stated earlier, even if you're not depressed and you just want to make a change in your life and lifestyle, these are success principles that can set you on the path to greatness and help you live the life of your dreams. God's desire is for you to live in a constant overflow of abundance, not barely making it, not surviving, but thriving! These are tools and techniques that can help you thrive and be truly happy, whole, joyful, and bouncing off the walls. God wants to re-introduce you to you. The new you. You're used to the hurt you, broken you, mad, sad, depressed, and angry you. The worrisome you. God wants to heal you totally and completely. He wants to introduce you to the happy you, whole you, funny you, the worry free you. The new you that you never thought you could be.

A funny story, when I was in high school I was so hard I did not like the color pink. It was just too soft, and I didn't want to be known as soft. I liked the color peach but not pink. I remember saying I could never wear pink. Well, after God got me together...my favorite color became pink! Light pink, dark pink, hot pink, I love all shades of pink! LOL! He can do the same for you. Change your nature and make you new. What's one thing you can do today to change your life? What's the one tool you can start today? I can honestly say that when I sit with myself quietly, I like me, and I love me. I no longer have any negative self-talk and the weight is lifted. Yes, I'm bouncing off the walls, giddy, happy, whole, and free. Now it's your turn! Get it! Your past doesn't have to hold your back anymore, your present is a gift and your future can be amazing. I never thought I could experience real joy, real laughter and real fun without feeling a weight on my chest. But I have!!I And you can too!

Know Who You Are And Whose You Are

It's vital for you to know who you are and whose you are. It's time for you to be the spiritual gangster that you are called to be. You are chosen of God to win in every area of your life. You don't have to be afraid of your dark side anymore. You are His child and He has your back. He created you to conquer! You are more than a conqueror because you win in the physical and spiritual world. So, If you don't already know I'm going to remind you that You are Strong. You are Powerful. You are Gifted. You are Special. You are Resilient and You are Called to Greatness! YES YOU! Could it be that the reason you're getting attacked is not because you're not supposed to be here but because you are called to greatness and you are called to reach so many people with your story! Your glory is through the story. So, walk on through. You are brave enough to see what's on the other side. Your past does not define. Your words do! There is a God that is for you and there's also an enemy against you. But, be encouraged because there is more for you than against you. God has given you the strength to fight, so use your weapons and win honey! He has given you the power to tread over every enemy and nothing shall by any means hurt you. You got this and God got you!

God is your refuge and you are your own rescue. Only you can make the quality decision to do the work! I declare you are no longer afraid of the dark. The dark is afraid of you!

CHAPTER 16
PRAYERS AND AFFIRMATIONS

I could not do any of this without a personal relationship with Jesus Christ. He gave me boldness and freedom when I chose to live for Him. Accept Him in your heart today.

Prayer of Salvation

God, I may not fully understand the life you have for me, but I know that you love me and Your plans for me will work out for my good. Jesus, I thank you for dying on the cross so that I can live. I ask you to forgive me of my sins, come into my heart, save my life and make me whole now. Fill me with your Holy Spirit and help me live everyday for you. I put myself--my life, my heart, my mind, my soul, my body and my future--in your hands. Create in me a clean heart and renew a right spirit in me so you can live through me and I can live for you forever. From this day forward I am happy, I am whole, I am free! In Jesus' Name, I pray Amen!

YAAAAAY YOU'RE SAVED!
WOOO HOOOOOOOOOOOOOO!!!!! :-))
Now find a local Bible based church to grow in. Go Often :)

DAILY AFFIRMATIONS for Women

You don't have to say all of them. Say the ones that stand out to you.

I am_____ (insert name here)
I am beautiful I am anointed I am strong, I am wise, I am confident I am a woman of God. I am fearless. I wear my crown.
I know who I am, whose I am and where I'm going. From this day forward, I will walk my journey fearlessly and with confidence because I know you walk beside me. I am courageous. I am brilliant. I am loving. I am loved. I am fearfully and wonderfully made by God. I am happy. I am whole I am complete.
I am a masterpiece. I am bold.
I am fearless. I am great. I am invincible. I defy all odds.
I am a winner. I always win. I am a great wife. I am great mother . I am a patient loving and kind wife and mom. I am in tuned to my family. I am a great friend. I am excellent. I am an excellent leader and CEO.
I am healthy and whole spirit soul and body. I think positive thoughts about myself and others. I pass every test at the top of my class. I am a billionaire now. I make billions of dollars now just being me. I am surrounded with greatness. I love passionately and I know I deserve love. I am wealthy I am prosperous I am rich. I AM ENOUGH!

I am so energetic! I am so vibrant. I am radiant. I am so creative I am a genius!

I spend time with God in His presence reading His word for direction and strength everyday.

I live in the overflow.

I am loving faithful and wise and I forgive myself and others quickly.

I am virtuous I am powerful and I am strong.

I am passionate and compassionate and sensitive to others needs

I speak kind words of life and love to myself to everyone around me.

I am a servant driven leader.

I am disciplined spirit soul and body.

I am proactive. I am highly focused on my dreams and goals.

I am in the best physical shape of my life.

My health is important to me.

I am highly organized.

I am very successful.

I am in the perfect will of God.

I am confident

I am financially responsible.

I attract God inspired ideas that produce billions of dollars now.

I am confident in the decisions that I make because I hear from God crystal clearly.

I finish what I start.

I believe in me. I am enough.

I AM ENOUGH!

I am so happy and grateful that money comes to me now quickly and easily in increasing quantities from multiple sources on a continuous basis now!

I get paid billions for being me.

Money comes to me frequently and easily now.

I am so blessed. I deserve to win I expect to win now!

I am blessed to be a blessing.

I am intentional about my actions.

I am consistent and diligent in the right things.

I am constantly motivated.

I'm empowered I'm strengthened I'm saturated with your word and presence and my soul is restored. I am Renewed daily.

My words are wise and I speak and give instructions with kindness

I am an expert in the message God has given me to share.

I am highly favored of God.

I am strong, I am energetic I am powerful.

I am highly successful.

Everything I touch prospers

I will never give up.

I am infused with a spirit of Success! I am successful

I am the best!

I attract wealth!

I am so creative

I'm the ultimate go getter

I am unique

I have crystal clear hearing on my goals and dreams

I see crystal clearly about my goals and Dreams.

I am the ultimate goal setter & go getter.

I receive money for good things!

Thank you Jesus!!

DAILY AFFIRMATIONS for men

I _____, (insert name here)

I am a strong wise , confident, anointed man of God.

I know who I am, whose I am and where I'm going.

From this day forward, I walk my journey fearlessly and
with confidence because I know You walk beside me.

I'm a man of love, joy, peace, wisdom, faith and
forgiveness.

I'm disciplined spirit soul and body.

I'm proactive. I'm highly focused on my dreams and goals.

I'm confident.

I'm in the best physical shape of my life.

I'm highly organized.

I'm successful.

I'm an excellent leader and CEO.

I'm known for my giving.

I'm in the perfect will of God.

I'm confident to speak in front of others.

I'm wealthy.

I attract God inspired ideas that produce millions of dollars.

I'm confident in the decisions that I make because I hear from God crystal clearly.

I'm intentional about my actions.

I'm consistent & diligent in the right things.

I'm constantly motivated.

I'm an expert in the message God has given me to share.

I'm highly favored of God.

I'm strong, energetic and powerful.

I'm highly successful

Everything I touch prospers

I will never give up.

Today I will be great! I will be intentional I will take massive action & I will get great results!

Today I give New Life to my Goals and Dreams!!

I'm infused with a spirit of Success!

I provide massive value in exchange for massive wealth!

Psalms 34: I sought you Lord and I thank you I am Healed and delivered out of all my fears. I look to you and I'm enlightened and my face is not ashamed. I thank you Lord that you're near me and you have healed my broken heart. Many are the afflictions of the righteous but you delivered me out of them all.

Isaiah 61: The spirit of the Lord is upon me, I thank you Lord that I have beauty for ashes, the oil of Joy for mourning and the garment of praise for the spirit of heaviness. And for my shame I receive double.

Psalm 27: One thing I desired of the Lord that I will continually seek, I will dwell in the House of the Lord all the days of my life to behold his beauty. In the day of trouble you shall hide me and keep me safe. Although my mother and father has forsaken me. You have taken me up and held me close and adopted me as your child. I am healed in Jesus Name. I am confident that I will see the goodness of the Lord, I wait on you Lord and I have good courage and you have strengthened my heart. Thank you.

Joshua 1:9 I am strong in the Lord and I have good courage and I know you're with me and have healed my broken heart. Thank you Jesus.

Col 2:10 I am complete and I have been brought to fullness in Jesus who is the head of all power and authority.

Psalms 62:5 My souls waits only upon God and silently submits to him, for my hope and expectation are from Him.

Psalms 119:130 The entrance of thy word gives light and understanding to the simple. Thank you for shining light on my darkness. I am free. I always win.

Also Read Psalms 23, 62, 63 and 84.

THANK YOU!

Thank you so much for reading my book! I pray it really blessed and transforms your life. I would love for you to connect with me on FB, IG, YouTube, and Twitter: Shantina Mullins and at Shantina.com

Please share your story and journey to wholeness and freedom with me. I would love to hear it! Email me at: iamshantina@gmail.com

Xoxo
Shantina*